Sundar Picnai

From Humble Beginnings to Google CEO
– Leadership, Innovation, and Life
Lessons

Clara Natasha

Table of Contents

Introduction

The Making of a Tech Visionary

In the world of modern technology, a select few individuals have left an indelible mark on the way we communicate, work, learn, and live. Among them stands Sundar Pichai—a quiet yet determined visionary whose rise from modest beginnings in Madurai, India, to the helm of one of the most powerful and influential companies on the planet is nothing short of extraordinary. His story is a powerful testament to the idea that no dream is too ambitious and no origin too humble to limit one's potential.

Born in a two-room apartment in the bustling city of Madurai, Sundar Pichai grew up in a household where resources were scarce but dreams were nurtured. His father, an electrical engineer, and his mother, a stenographer, instilled in him the values of curiosity, hard work, and resilience—qualities that would later become the cornerstone of his leadership philosophy. Even as a child, Pichai exhibited an innate fascination for technology, an early sign of the transformative path his life would eventually take.

Education was Pichai's gateway to the world beyond his immediate surroundings. His journey led him from the Indian Institute of Technology in Kharagpur to Stanford University and finally to the Wharton School at the University of Pennsylvania, where he honed both his technical expertise and business acumen. But his story is not simply one of academic achievement; it is a story of relentless curiosity, quiet determination, and a deep belief in the power of ideas and collaboration.

When Pichai joined Google in 2004, the tech world was beginning to expand at an unprecedented pace. His early contributions—particularly his work on the Google Toolbar and the groundbreaking development of the Chrome browser—showcased his unique blend of technical brilliance and user-focused design thinking. Chrome's success not only disrupted the internet browsing landscape but also highlighted Pichai's ability to anticipate market needs and execute large-scale projects with precision and vision.

As the chapters of his professional life unfolded, Pichai demonstrated time and again the qualities of a transformative leader. His ascent through the ranks at Google was marked not by self-promotion or aggressive ambition but by empathy, collaboration, and an unshakable focus on long-term goals. Whether guiding the Android team, spearheading the evolution of Google's core products, or leading the charge into artificial intelligence and cloud computing, Pichai's leadership style remained consistent— measured, thoughtful, and people-centric.

In 2015, when Google underwent a major corporate restructuring to form its parent company, Alphabet Inc., Pichai was named CEO of Google—a role that placed him at the center of the global tech conversation. By 2019, he assumed the mantle of CEO for Alphabet as well, becoming one of the most influential figures in technology and business. Despite the towering nature of his responsibilities, Pichai remained grounded, consistently advocating for the responsible use of technology and emphasizing ethical innovation in an increasingly complex digital world.

Beyond his professional accomplishments, Sundar Pichai's life offers profound lessons in humility, adaptability, and perseverance. His journey reminds us that leadership is not defined by volume or bravado but by the quiet strength to listen, the wisdom to adapt, and the courage to forge ahead, even in the face of uncertainty. He embodies the idea that success is not confined to those born with privilege but is accessible to those who approach life with curiosity, compassion, and a commitment to lifelong learning.

This biography, Sundar Pichai: From Humble Beginnings to Google CEO – Leadership, Innovation, and Life Lessons, invites readers to explore the extraordinary story behind a man who transformed the way billions of people interact with technology. Each chapter sheds light on his early influences, his approach to innovation, and the leadership philosophies that have defined his journey. It is a story of resilience, vision, and purpose—a story that proves greatness can rise from the most unassuming of places.

Prepare to embark on a journey that not only charts the professional milestones of Sundar Pichai but also reveals the mindset and values that propelled him from the streets of Madurai to the boardrooms of Silicon Valley. His life is more than just a success story; it is an inspiration for anyone daring to dream beyond their circumstances.

Chapter 1

Roots in Madurai – Early Life and Family

Long before Sundar Pichai would stand on the grand stages of global technology conferences, long before his name would become synonymous with Google and innovation, his story began in the heart of southern India—in the historic city of Madurai. Known for its vibrant temples, age-old traditions, and a deep-rooted sense of community, Madurai was a place where culture and simplicity walked hand in hand. It was here, amidst the bustling streets and the hum of everyday life, that Pichai Sundararajan, later known to the world as Sundar Pichai, was born on June 10, 1972.

Sundar's early years were marked by modesty. His family lived in a small, two-room apartment, located in an ordinary neighborhood. Their home was not defined by luxury or material abundance, but it was rich in warmth, discipline, and encouragement. His father, Regunatha Pichai, worked as an electrical engineer at GEC, the British conglomerate, while his mother, Lakshmi, was a stenographer before she chose to focus on raising Sundar and his younger brother.

His father played a particularly influential role in sparking Sundar's early curiosity about technology. Regunatha Pichai often brought home stories from his workplace, talking about the components, machinery, and systems he worked on. Although their family budget did not allow for many modern conveniences—owning a television, telephone, or even a car were luxuries beyond reach at the time—what the Pichai household did have was an endless supply of intellectual encouragement. Sundar grew up watching his father tinker with electrical devices, fix household electronics, and explain complex technical problems in a way that was both fascinating and accessible. These early experiences laid the foundation for a mind naturally inclined toward analytical thinking and problem-solving.

Life in Madurai was simple but structured. The Pichai family placed a strong emphasis on education, discipline, and self-reliance. Resources might have been limited, but imagination, effort, and integrity were abundant. This value system, deeply embedded in Sundar's upbringing, became a guiding force throughout his life.

As a child, Sundar attended Jawahar Vidyalaya, a modest school in Chennai, where his academic talents began to emerge. Even during these early years, he showed a keen interest in numbers, patterns, and logic—traits that would later define his approach to both technology and leadership. His teachers would often describe him as soft-spoken yet highly observant, someone who rarely sought the spotlight but always delivered excellence in his work.

One fascinating and often-quoted detail from his childhood was his remarkable memory, particularly when it came to remembering telephone numbers. In a time when few homes in his neighborhood even had a telephone, Sundar developed an ability to memorize and recall long strings of numbers with ease—a skill that, while simple on the surface, hinted at his powerful capacity for information processing and attention to detail.

Outside the classroom, Sundar's upbringing was shaped by a blend of traditional Indian values and the evolving culture of a country on the brink of technological and economic transformation. Madurai, with its centuries-old temples and deeply spiritual atmosphere, instilled in him an appreciation for history, community, and resilience. At the same time, the technological conversations at home, along with India's emerging focus on science and engineering education, exposed him to a world of innovation and progress.

Sundar's pathway to higher education was a reflection of his quiet determination. After excelling in school, he earned a coveted seat at the Indian Institute of Technology (IIT) Kharagpur, one of the most prestigious and competitive engineering schools in India. There, he pursued Metallurgical Engineering, though his interest always extended far beyond his chosen field. Professors and peers alike noted his sharp intellect and thoughtful approach to problem-solving, a combination that set him apart even in a sea of gifted students.

During his time at IIT, Sundar's worldview expanded beyond the classroom. The friendships he forged, the challenges he embraced, and the late-night conversations about technology and global affairs all contributed to shaping a young man who was both grounded and globally aware. His academic excellence and intellectual curiosity earned him a scholarship to Stanford University in the United States—a milestone that would mark the beginning of his transformation from a bright student from Madurai into a global technology leader.

However, it is important to understand that Sundar's success was not simply the result of academic achievement or professional opportunities. It was his upbringing—the quiet lessons learned in a small apartment in Madurai, the observation of a father's meticulous engineering work, the encouragement of a mother's unwavering belief in education, and the values of humility, integrity, and hard work—that truly shaped his character. These formative years built a strong foundation upon which all of his future achievements would rest.

The story of Sundar Pichai's early life is a story of contrasts. A life where material scarcity met intellectual abundance. A life where cultural heritage met curiosity for the future. And above all, a life where humility stood side by side with ambition.

For anyone looking to understand the leader Sundar Pichai would become, it is essential to first understand the young boy from Madurai—the boy who grew up with no grand expectations of global fame, but with a quiet commitment to learning, adapting, and contributing meaningfully to the world. His early years shaped not only his career but his worldview, teaching him the value of patience, empathy, and the art of listening— traits that would later become hallmarks of his leadership style at Google and beyond.

As we leave the humble streets of Madurai and follow Sundar's journey across continents, from the classrooms of IIT to the corporate campuses of Silicon Valley, one truth remains constant: his roots have always kept him grounded, serving as a powerful reminder that success is built not only on talent but on values nurtured from the very beginning.

Chapter 2

Academic Excellence – From IIT Kharagpur to Wharton

The road to greatness is often paved by a relentless commitment to learning, and for Sundar Pichai, that path began to take clear shape during his academic journey—a journey that would stretch from the classrooms of India's most prestigious engineering institute to the lecture halls of America's finest universities.

After an impressive performance throughout his schooling years in Chennai, Pichai earned a coveted seat at the Indian Institute of Technology (IIT) Kharagpur, one of the most competitive and distinguished educational institutions in the country. For generations, IITs have stood as the benchmark of academic excellence in India, admitting only the most brilliant minds after a grueling and highly selective entrance examination process. The achievement alone was a testament to Sundar's intellectual capacity, discipline, and deep-rooted passion for problem-solving.

At IIT Kharagpur, Sundar enrolled in the Department of Metallurgical Engineering. While the choice of specialization might seem unexpected for someone who would eventually reshape the digital technology landscape, his years at IIT were anything but limited to metallurgy. Sundar displayed not only academic brilliance but also a wide-ranging curiosity that stretched beyond his textbooks.

His professors quickly took note of his thoughtfulness, technical insight, and ability to approach complex problems from fresh angles. More than just memorizing facts or formulas, Sundar possessed an instinct for simplifying challenges into their core components—a skill that would later define his product design and leadership at Google. Those who studied alongside him often recalled how calm and unassuming he was, even in moments of high pressure. Whether he was participating in technical discussions, working on a group project, or sitting for an exam, Sundar exuded quiet confidence and intellectual clarity.

During his time at IIT, Pichai also became aware of the importance of collaboration and global thinking. While his roots were deeply Indian, the influence of India's growing interest in software and technology during the early 1990s piqued his desire to understand innovation on a worldwide scale. His thirst for knowledge extended beyond metallurgy—he was keenly interested in computer science, design thinking, and emerging technologies that were beginning to reshape industries far beyond India's borders.

Recognizing his outstanding potential, Sundar was awarded a scholarship to Stanford University, one of the world's leading institutions for science and technology research. For the young man from Madurai, this was more than an academic milestone—it was a transformative life event. Leaving India and arriving in the heart of Silicon Valley, Sundar found himself surrounded by the sharpest minds, cutting-edge ideas, and a culture that celebrated experimentation and risk-taking.

At Stanford, he pursued a Master of Science in Material Sciences and Engineering, diving deep into advanced materials, nanotechnology, and semiconductor physics. The technical rigor of Stanford further sharpened his analytical skills, but it was the environment of intellectual freedom and collaboration that left the deepest imprint on him. Here, Sundar learned to blend his strong engineering foundation with a growing understanding of user-centric design, business innovation, and global impact.

Stanford's campus offered more than just academic excellence—it exposed Pichai to the entrepreneurial spirit that defines Silicon Valley. Conversations about start-ups, new software platforms, and product prototypes were as common as casual coffee breaks. The atmosphere encouraged students to think beyond existing frameworks, to ask "what if" and "why not" rather than settle for the way things had always been done. This mindset left a lasting impression on Sundar, shaping the way he would later lead innovation at Google.

Even after completing his master's degree, Pichai's hunger for learning didn't end. Wanting to complement his technical knowledge with business expertise, Sundar enrolled at the Wharton School of the University of Pennsylvania, one of the most prestigious business schools in the world. At

Wharton, he pursued an MBA, and once again, his quiet excellence earned him recognition—this time in the form of the Siebel Scholar and Palmer Scholar distinctions, honors awarded to the top-performing students in the class.

At Wharton, Pichai learned the language of business strategy, organizational leadership, and decision-making at scale. The structured yet dynamic business education allowed him to see the intersection between technology and human behavior, understanding not only how products are built, but how they are adopted, scaled, and improved through user feedback and market forces. It was here that Pichai strengthened his ability to balance the human and technical sides of business—a skill that would later allow him to navigate Google's complex ecosystem of products, services, and global users.

Looking back, it becomes clear that Pichai's academic journey was more than a series of degrees or institutions—it was a transformational process of shaping both intellect and character. From the disciplined classrooms of IIT Kharagpur to the research labs at Stanford, and finally to the strategic boardrooms of Wharton, each stage of his education played a role in preparing him for the extraordinary challenges and opportunities that lay ahead.

These experiences refined more than just his technical skills; they shaped his leadership philosophy. Sundar learned the importance of listening before speaking, of observing before acting, and of making decisions rooted in both data and empathy. His calm, methodical approach to problem-solving was born in the academic rigor of IIT, elevated at Stanford, and rounded out at Wharton, where business and human understanding came into sharp focus.

What makes his academic journey so remarkable is not just where he studied, but how he approached learning itself. At every stage, Sundar's success was defined by humility, a love of inquiry, and an unshakable commitment to personal growth. These were the lessons that would one day guide him as he led global teams, made billion-dollar decisions, and shaped the future of one of the world's most influential companies.

His journey from Madurai to Silicon Valley serves as a powerful reminder: knowledge is the foundation upon which dreams are built, and education—when embraced with sincerity and purpose—can open doors that stretch far beyond imagination.

Chapter 3

The Silicon Valley Leap – Joining Google

For many aspiring engineers and innovators, Silicon Valley is not merely a geographical location — it is a symbol of possibility, a place where ideas are born, tested, and scaled to change the world. For Sundar Pichai, the journey from a modest two-room apartment in Madurai to the cutting-edge offices of Silicon Valley had been paved with determination, discipline, and a relentless thirst for knowledge. Now, armed with advanced degrees from Stanford University and the Wharton School, Pichai stood at the crossroads of academic accomplishment and real-world innovation.

The early 2000s were a defining era in the world of technology. The dot-com bubble had burst, yet companies were rebuilding stronger and smarter. The internet was evolving from static webpages into dynamic, user-driven platforms, and a quiet revolution was underway — one that would eventually redefine industries and societies alike. In the heart of this technological transformation stood a young company named Google.

Founded in 1998 by Larry Page and Sergey Brin, Google was still in its growth phase in the early 2000s. The company had already started reshaping how people accessed information, but it was clear that the future held even greater possibilities. In 2004, Sundar Pichai joined Google — a decision that would not only change the trajectory of his own life but also the path of the company itself.

At first glance, Pichai's move to Google might have seemed like a conventional choice for a tech-savvy engineer equipped with a stellar academic background. But the decision was anything but simple. At the time, Google was a young, ambitious company competing in an ever-expanding market. Joining Google meant stepping into an environment known for high expectations, intellectual rigor, and a culture that challenged every assumption — a place where only the most adaptive and forward-thinking individuals thrived.

Pichai joined Google as part of the product management team. His initial assignment was deceptively simple: oversee and improve the Google Toolbar. In the early 2000s, the Toolbar was a crucial feature that allowed users to search Google directly from their web browser without visiting the search engine's homepage. Though the Toolbar might not have seemed revolutionary on the surface, Pichai recognized the deeper implications of user convenience and the growing intersection between browsers and search engines.

It was during this period that he began to demonstrate the qualities that would eventually make him a standout leader:

sharp analytical thinking, a collaborative spirit, and an uncanny ability to focus on the end-user experience. Rather than looking at products as isolated tools, Pichai approached them as part of a broader ecosystem — an approach that set him apart in Google's problem-solving culture.

One of the defining moments of his early career at Google came when he championed the idea of developing Google's own web browser. At the time, Microsoft's Internet Explorer dominated the market, and the idea of competing against such an entrenched player was considered both risky and ambitious. Many insiders were skeptical, questioning whether a search engine company had any business developing a browser.

But Pichai saw the future unfolding differently. He recognized that browsers were the gateway to the internet, and that Google's success as a search and services platform would increasingly depend on the performance, flexibility, and security of the browsing experience. He argued that controlling the browser would allow Google to innovate faster, protect user privacy more effectively, and optimize the way its services integrated across platforms.

Convincing the leadership team, including co-founders Larry Page and Sergey Brin, to back this vision was no small feat. But Pichai's calm, data-backed reasoning and his deep understanding of both the technical and strategic dimensions of the issue ultimately swayed them. The result was the launch of Google Chrome in 2008.

Chrome wasn't just another web browser; it was a statement. It offered faster page loading, a clean and minimalist interface, and groundbreaking features like isolated tabs that improved both stability and security. Under Pichai's guidance, Chrome evolved from an internal experiment to a product that rapidly captured global market share, becoming the world's most popular web browser.

This success cemented Pichai's reputation as a visionary product leader. But it was not just his technical insights that stood out — it was his leadership style. In a culture known for intense debate and strong personalities, Pichai remained calm, composed, and respectful. He listened more than he spoke, fostered collaboration instead of competition, and always kept the focus on users rather than internal politics.

As Chrome's success grew, so did Pichai's responsibilities. He was soon entrusted with overseeing some of Google's most critical and influential products, including Gmail, Google Drive, and Google Maps. Each product presented new challenges: maintaining simplicity while scaling to millions (and then billions) of users, balancing innovation with reliability, and navigating the rapidly shifting technological landscape.

His growing portfolio reflected the deep trust Google's leadership had in him. Whether guiding the development of Android — the world's most widely used mobile operating system — or shaping the future of cloud computing, Pichai approached every challenge with the same clarity and composure that had defined his early days at the company.

His ability to unify teams around a common vision, make complex technical decisions accessible, and maintain a steady hand in the face of uncertainty earned him admiration not only from his peers but also from the founders of Google themselves. Over time, he became a central figure in shaping Google's strategy, culture, and direction.

Looking back, Sundar Pichai's decision to join Google in 2004 was more than a career move — it was the beginning of a lifelong mission to make technology accessible, useful, and transformative for people around the world. The challenges he faced along the way, from navigating product skepticism to leading under pressure, honed the leadership qualities that would one day prepare him for the highest seat at Google and, later, its parent company, Alphabet.

In many ways, his early years at Google mirrored his approach to life: embrace challenges with humility, stay committed to learning, and lead with empathy and purpose. These principles would continue to define both his career and his enduring influence on the world of technology.

Chapter 4

Pioneering Products – Chrome, Android, and Beyond

In the world of technology, innovation is often measured not just by groundbreaking ideas but by the ability to transform those ideas into products that impact the lives of millions — or even billions — of people. Sundar Pichai's journey at Google is a masterclass in exactly that: taking vision and curiosity and translating them into practical tools that shape the digital landscape.

By the time Pichai had settled into his early roles at Google, it was clear that his influence would stretch far beyond any one assignment. He brought to the company a rare combination of engineering excellence, thoughtful leadership, and an ability to anticipate future trends, all of which would soon converge in the development of one of the most influential products in internet history: Google Chrome.

The Birth of Google Chrome: Reimagining the Gateway to the Web

When Sundar Pichai first began advocating for Google to build its own web browser, the idea seemed audacious. The early 2000s web ecosystem was dominated by Microsoft's Internet Explorer, which had become the default browsing tool for the majority of the world's internet users. For a search engine company to enter this arena seemed risky at best and reckless at worst.

But Pichai possessed a keen sense of observation. He recognized that as the web evolved from static pages to dynamic applications, the browser would no longer be a simple tool for navigation — it would become the very platform upon which most digital experiences were built. Websites were increasingly acting like full-fledged applications, requiring browsers to handle heavier loads, execute complex scripts, and manage multiple tasks without compromising performance or security.

With characteristic calm and precision, Pichai laid out his case to Google's leadership, highlighting the importance of controlling the "user entry point" to the internet. He emphasized the potential to create a browser that was faster, more secure, and more intuitive — a browser designed not for the web of yesterday, but for the internet of the future.

The result of this vision was Google Chrome, launched in 2008. More than just a new browser, Chrome embodied an entirely new philosophy of user-centered design and engineering efficiency. Features like tab isolation, automatic updates, and a minimalist interface stripped away distractions and placed performance and security at the heart of the browsing experience.

Under Pichai's leadership, Chrome quickly distinguished itself from its competitors. Its speed and simplicity won users over, and its commitment to open-source development via the Chromium project fueled a growing ecosystem of innovation. Within a few years, Chrome displaced long-time giants in the market, becoming the world's most widely used web browser.

But perhaps more important than market share was what Chrome symbolized: a shift in Google's ambitions from being a company that helped people find information to one that actively shaped how people experienced the web itself. This shift was not accidental; it was the product of Pichai's quiet but resolute leadership, his belief in thoughtful problem-solving, and his ability to motivate teams to focus on long-term impact over short-term gains.

The Android Revolution: Expanding Google's Reach to Every Pocket

Pichai's success with Chrome had firmly established his reputation within Google. It wasn't long before the company tapped him for another pivotal role — this time overseeing Android, the open-source mobile operating system that was quietly rewriting the rules of the mobile industry.

When Pichai took over Android in 2013, the mobile operating system had already achieved significant market penetration, but it still faced stiff competition, especially from Apple's iOS ecosystem. Pichai's approach was both pragmatic and visionary. He believed that Android's strength lay in its openness and adaptability. Under his guidance, Android evolved to become more than just an operating system — it became the foundation for a vast and vibrant global ecosystem of developers, device makers, and users.

One of Pichai's most profound insights was understanding the mobile device not as a standalone product but as a gateway to an interconnected world. Whether it was through Google's suite of apps, cloud services, or machine learning-backed features, Android devices were positioned to provide users with seamless experiences that crossed borders, platforms, and languages.

Pichai was also instrumental in driving Android's expansion beyond smartphones. His leadership encouraged new partnerships with hardware manufacturers, resulting in the spread of Android to tablets, wearables, cars, televisions, and smart home devices — effectively embedding Google's presence in every corner of modern digital life.

His work on Android not only strengthened Google's position in the mobile industry but also helped democratize access to technology across the world. Android's open-source nature made it possible for manufacturers to build devices at varying price points, enabling millions of people, especially in emerging markets, to join the digital age.

Beyond Chrome and Android: Cultivating an Innovation-First Culture

While Chrome and Android are often the headliners in discussions about Pichai's achievements, his influence at Google extended to many other groundbreaking products and initiatives. He played a guiding role in the ongoing evolution of Google Drive, Gmail, Google Maps, and Google Photos — services that have become staples of everyday digital life.

Each of these products followed a similar blueprint: focus on solving real-world problems, prioritize user experience, and never settle for "good enough" when excellence is possible. Whether it was rethinking how people manage their emails, simplifying cloud storage for billions, or improving global navigation through accurate and dynamic mapping, Pichai's fingerprints were on some of the most transformative products in Google's portfolio.

One of his defining traits as a leader was his quiet insistence on collaboration. Pichai believed that innovation was not the work of a single genius but the result of collective curiosity and shared purpose. He created spaces where teams felt empowered to take calculated risks, learn from failures, and return stronger with better solutions. His low-ego leadership style inspired loyalty and creativity, and helped foster a culture where even the most ambitious ideas could take shape and thrive.

A Vision for the Future

The products that Sundar Pichai helped build — Chrome, Android, and the broader Google ecosystem — did more than change user habits. They reshaped industries, challenged conventions, and opened new frontiers of possibility. In each case, Pichai's influence was clear: an unwavering focus on the user, a commitment to technical excellence, and a leadership style grounded in humility and long-term thinking.

As the digital world continues to evolve, the foundations laid by these products still serve as guideposts for the future of technology. Whether it's enabling global communication, expanding access to information, or improving the way humans interact with machines, Pichai's work has left an indelible mark on the modern world.

Through these successes, Pichai demonstrated that true innovation is not a single moment of brilliance but a continuous cycle of observation, empathy, experimentation, and execution. His career serves as a powerful reminder that with curiosity, collaboration, and quiet determination, even the most ambitious dreams can become reality.

Chapter 5

Rising to the Top – Becoming Google CEO

Sundar Pichai's journey from a young boy in Madurai to the CEO of one of the world's most influential companies is the embodiment of the transformative power of leadership, innovation, and vision. As he rose through the ranks at Google, his leadership style, grounded in humility and an unwavering focus on the long-term, propelled him from overseeing the development of Google's core products to eventually leading the entire company.

Pichai's ascent within Google was a steady and methodical climb, but it was not without challenges. By the time he was named the CEO of Google in 2015, he had already established himself as one of the most trusted executives at the company. His ability to lead large, diverse teams, coupled with his keen sense of product development and business strategy, positioned him as the ideal candidate to steer Google into its next chapter.

The Role of a Leader: Building Trust and Driving Innovation

Sundar's leadership journey at Google was marked by his ability to align technology with human needs, crafting products and services that enhanced lives while maintaining the company's core mission of making information universally accessible and useful. His focus was always on building products that could scale to millions — or even billions — of people, and he was adamant that this should never come at the expense of simplicity or ease of use.

As he took on more responsibility within Google, Pichai's leadership style became defined by several key principles:

1. Empathy for the User – In every product, initiative, or decision, Pichai emphasized the importance of user-centric thinking. His leadership was marked by a deep understanding that technology should be empowering, not intimidating. Whether it was improving the accessibility of Google Maps or ensuring Gmail's interface was intuitive for people of all ages and backgrounds, Pichai's focus remained on delivering a seamless and thoughtful user experience.

2. Collaboration Over Competition – Pichai's calm demeanor and collaborative spirit stood in stark contrast to the competitive, high-energy environment that often characterizes Silicon Valley. Rather than vying for recognition, Sundar fostered a work culture

that valued teamwork and collaboration. He was known for encouraging his teams to take risks, make mistakes, and learn quickly from their failures. This approach allowed Google to maintain its innovative edge while continually pushing the envelope on what was possible.

3. Long-Term Vision – While many tech leaders are often consumed with quarterly results, Pichai always seemed more focused on the future. He understood that the big ideas that would define Google for decades were not the ones that could be realized in a year or two. Instead, Pichai focused on positioning Google for success over the long haul, making investments in areas such as artificial intelligence, cloud computing, and hardware — all while maintaining a clear focus on the company's core values of accessibility, transparency, and simplicity.

4. Quiet Confidence – One of the most striking things about Pichai as a leader was his quiet, almost reserved demeanor. In a world where flamboyant CEOs often dominate the headlines, Pichai stood out for his ability to lead without the need for constant attention or drama. His calm and composed presence in the face of adversity set a tone of stability and confidence for the entire company.

By 2014, it was becoming increasingly clear that Pichai's influence within Google was growing. He had successfully steered the development of some of the company's most important products, and his leadership had helped solidify Google's position as the dominant player in the tech industry. It was also around this time that Pichai began to take on more high-profile roles within the company, overseeing not only Google's core products but also strategic areas like Android, Chrome, and apps.

The Alphabet Reshuffle: A New Era for Google

In August 2015, a major restructuring took place at Google. Larry Page and Sergey Brin, the company's founders, made the bold decision to create Alphabet Inc., a new corporate structure that would house Google as one of its subsidiaries while giving the company more flexibility to diversify into other industries. This marked a new chapter for Google, one where it could continue its relentless focus on its core search and advertising businesses while also exploring areas like health, robotics, and self-driving cars.

In the wake of this transformation, Sundar Pichai was named the CEO of Google. The move was widely seen as a natural progression for Pichai, given his deep knowledge of the company, his strategic acumen, and his reputation for calm and effective leadership. It also represented a shift in the company's leadership — from the founding duo of Page and Brin, who had steered Google through its early, explosive growth, to a new generation of leaders tasked with continuing Google's legacy while managing its immense global reach.

Pichai's appointment as CEO of Google also highlighted the shift in priorities for the company. Whereas in the early days, Google had been primarily focused on search and ads, under Pichai's leadership, the company began to place more emphasis on artificial intelligence, cloud computing, and hardware, areas that would define the company's next chapter.

Leading Google Into the Future

As CEO, Sundar Pichai faced an environment that was both exciting and fraught with challenges. Google had already reached monumental heights, but the road ahead was anything but predictable. The tech industry was rapidly evolving, with new competitors emerging in every corner of the market. Meanwhile, Google itself was faced with increasing scrutiny from regulators and consumers, who were becoming more concerned about issues like privacy, data security, and the ethics of artificial intelligence.

However, Pichai's steady hand and forward-thinking leadership ensured that Google not only navigated these challenges but also thrived in the face of them. Under his leadership, the company doubled down on its commitment to artificial intelligence (AI), and Pichai became one of the most vocal advocates for the potential of AI to improve lives. He championed initiatives that would put AI at the center of Google's future, from improving search algorithms to enhancing the capabilities of the Google Assistant, Google's voice-activated AI system.

One of his first big moves as CEO was to strengthen Google's focus on cloud computing. Recognizing that cloud services were rapidly becoming the backbone of modern enterprise IT, Pichai pushed for Google Cloud to compete with the likes of Amazon Web Services (AWS) and Microsoft Azure. His efforts in this space helped cement Google's position as a major player in the cloud industry, providing businesses with scalable, secure, and innovative cloud-based tools.

Pichai also led Google's push into hardware. Under his guidance, the company introduced a range of consumer hardware products, from the Pixel smartphone to Google Home smart speakers. These products, while not always the market leader, represented a strategic attempt by Google to not just dominate the software and services space but also to integrate its ecosystem into the physical world.

Despite the increasing challenges of managing one of the world's largest companies, Pichai never lost sight of what made Google unique — its mission to make information accessible and useful. Whether it was providing new ways for people to connect with others, or empowering businesses to thrive in the digital age, Pichai's focus remained on using technology as a force for good.

Legacy and Impact

Sundar Pichai's rise to the position of Google CEO is not just a story of personal success; it is the story of a leader who has shaped the future of technology itself. From his beginnings in Madurai to becoming the head of a company that influences nearly every aspect of the modern digital experience, Pichai's journey is a testament to the power of perseverance, curiosity, and a focus on long-term vision.

As CEO of Google, Pichai continues to lead with a quiet confidence that inspires those around him. His leadership is characterized by his ability to focus on the bigger picture, adapt to an ever-changing industry, and lead with empathy. The world may have changed since he first joined Google in 2004, but Sundar Pichai's approach to leadership — grounded in integrity, innovation, and a commitment to improving lives — remains as powerful as ever.

Chapter 6

Leading Alphabet – Vision for the Future

Sundar Pichai's ascent to the position of CEO of Alphabet was a natural progression for a leader who had already proven himself within the world of Google. However, becoming the CEO of Alphabet, Google's parent company, marked a new chapter in his leadership journey — one where his vision for the future would shape the direction of not just Google, but an entire conglomerate with interests ranging from technology to life sciences. As the steward of Alphabet, Pichai was tasked with leading a company that was not only one of the largest and most powerful tech entities in the world but one that had also diversified into groundbreaking fields such as artificial intelligence (AI), autonomous vehicles, and healthcare.

Under Pichai's leadership, Alphabet began to shift its focus from merely being a digital advertising powerhouse to a company whose vision extends far beyond the screen. As the world's most powerful tech company, Alphabet is uniquely positioned to influence the trajectory of human progress. And Sundar Pichai's ability to craft a strategic vision that includes both the company's core strengths and its new frontiers is a testament to his foresight, innovation, and deep understanding of global trends.

A Bold Vision for Artificial Intelligence

One of the most prominent areas where Sundar Pichai has steered Alphabet's future is in artificial intelligence (AI). Under his leadership, Alphabet has made substantial investments in AI, recognizing its transformative potential to revolutionize industries ranging from healthcare to education to entertainment. Pichai has consistently argued that AI is perhaps the most important technological development in human history, capable of solving complex challenges and improving lives in ways that were previously unimaginable.

Alphabet's flagship AI-driven initiatives began to take shape as Google Brain, which developed deep learning techniques, and Google DeepMind, an AI research lab. One of DeepMind's most celebrated accomplishments was the creation of AlphaGo, an AI that defeated world champions in the ancient game of Go — a feat once thought to be impossible for machines. This achievement signaled not just the capabilities of AI but also its potential to address complex problem-solving challenges in the real world.

Under Pichai's leadership, Alphabet made AI the centerpiece of its global strategy. In 2018, Pichai unveiled Google AI, a division focused on accelerating the company's AI capabilities while ensuring its responsible use. His vision was clear: AI should be deployed to improve user experiences, drive business solutions, and solve societal challenges, all while being handled ethically and transparently.

Beyond Google Search, Pichai has emphasized the role of AI in products such as Google Assistant, which leverages AI to create a personalized and seamless experience for users. Google Cloud's AI and machine learning services have also emerged as powerful tools for businesses to optimize operations, automate tasks, and unlock insights from vast amounts of data. Under Pichai, Alphabet has also launched several initiatives aimed at democratizing AI, including the Google AI for Social Good program, which uses AI to address societal issues like natural disasters, health disparities, and more.

Pichai has repeatedly emphasized that while AI is a powerful tool, it is crucial to develop and deploy it responsibly. To this end,

Alphabet has made major strides in setting ethical guidelines for AI research, ensuring fairness, transparency, and accountability in its application. Pichai's commitment to the responsible use of AI underscores his understanding that technology, in the wrong hands or used without foresight, can do more harm than good.

Sustainability: Paving the Path for a Green Future

Another area where Sundar Pichai has made a significant impact is in sustainability. As a global leader in the tech industry, Alphabet has the power to set the standard for environmentally conscious business practices. Pichai has been a strong advocate for the idea that technology and sustainability need not be at odds. In fact, he believes that technological innovation can, and should, play a central role in addressing the most pressing environmental challenges facing the planet.

One of Pichai's most notable achievements in this area is Alphabet's commitment to sustainability. Since 2007, Google has been carbon-neutral, meaning it has offset its carbon emissions through initiatives like renewable energy purchases and carbon credits. However, under Pichai's leadership, Alphabet has taken these efforts a step further. In 2020, Alphabet made an ambitious pledge to achieve carbon-free energy by 2030, a goal that extends beyond just reducing carbon emissions to creating a world where the company's entire global operations run on renewable energy — without the need for carbon offsets.

This commitment to sustainability also extends to Alphabet's subsidiary companies. Waymo, the company's autonomous vehicle arm, is working on creating self-driving cars that could reduce traffic congestion and lower carbon emissions by enabling more efficient transportation. Loon, which uses high-altitude balloons to deliver internet access to remote regions, is another example of Alphabet's dedication to innovative solutions that address both environmental and societal issues.

Additionally, Alphabet has been investing in sustainable products and services, including Google's ongoing efforts to make its hardware products, such as Pixel phones and Nest thermostats, more environmentally friendly. By 2022, Google had launched its Circular Economy initiative, a program focused on using recycled materials, reducing waste, and creating products designed for reuse.

Pichai's approach to sustainability goes beyond corporate responsibility. He understands that climate change and environmental degradation are global issues that require collective action. Alphabet's focus on sustainability is not only about reducing its own carbon footprint but about using its platform to inspire other companies, industries, and even governments to follow suit.

Global Expansion: Bridging the Digital Divide

Pichai's vision for Alphabet also includes a deep commitment to global expansion, particularly in regions that have historically been underserved by technology. Under his leadership, Alphabet has worked tirelessly to bring internet access to remote parts of the world and connect people who are still without reliable access to the internet.

Through projects like Project Loon, which uses balloons to provide internet to remote areas, and Google Station, which aims to bring high-speed Wi-Fi to public spaces in developing countries, Alphabet is tackling the digital divide head-on. These initiatives are part of a broader vision that Sundar

Pichai has for Alphabet's role in building a more connected, equitable world.

Pichai's deep roots in India have undoubtedly shaped his view on global expansion. Growing up in a country where access to technology was limited in many rural areas, Pichai has always been keenly aware of the power of connectivity in transforming lives. Alphabet's push to expand its digital services to emerging markets reflects his belief that the benefits of the digital revolution should be accessible to all.

Alphabet's Investments in the Future

As the CEO of Alphabet, Sundar Pichai is not only leading the company's existing operations but also positioning it for the future. Pichai has spearheaded Alphabet's strategic investments in a range of emerging technologies that are set to define the next wave of innovation. Among these are quantum computing, biotech and healthcare innovations, and advanced robotics.

One of the most high-profile investments Alphabet has made under Pichai is in quantum computing. While quantum computers are still in the early stages of development, they hold the potential to revolutionize fields ranging from cryptography to medicine. Google's Quantum AI team, under Pichai's leadership, made headlines in 2019 when it announced that it had achieved quantum supremacy — a milestone that demonstrated that quantum computers could perform calculations that would be practically impossible for classical computers.

In the field of biotechnology and healthcare, Alphabet's subsidiary Verily is working on projects aimed at solving complex medical challenges. Verily is exploring everything from smart contact lenses that measure glucose levels to innovative solutions for tracking and predicting diseases. Sundar Pichai's vision for Alphabet's role in healthcare is clear: by combining AI with deep scientific research, Alphabet can play a pivotal role in improving global health outcomes.

In the realm of advanced robotics, Pichai has overseen Alphabet's acquisition of several robotics companies, positioning Alphabet as a potential leader in automation technology. Whether in factories or in healthcare settings, the future of robotics promises to be a game-changer for industries and everyday life.

The Legacy of Sundar Pichai: A Visionary Leader

Sundar Pichai's leadership at Alphabet is defined by his commitment to pushing the boundaries of what technology can achieve, while remaining grounded in the belief that innovation should serve humanity. Through his work in AI, sustainability, global expansion, and emerging technologies, Pichai is not only guiding one of the world's most influential companies but shaping the future of technology itself.

As Alphabet looks toward the future, Pichai's steady leadership will continue to guide the company toward greater heights. His vision is clear: a future where technology works for everyone, where AI enhances lives, and where the digital divide is bridged. Sundar Pichai is not just leading Alphabet into the future — he is helping to create it.

Chapter 7

Leadership Philosophy – Empathy, Innovation, and Integrity

Sundar Pichai's leadership philosophy is one that combines empathy, innovation, and integrity, three core values that he believes are fundamental to fostering a culture of success, creativity, and ethical responsibility. Pichai's approach to leadership is not just about driving results or executing business strategies — it's about cultivating an environment where people are encouraged to grow, think creatively, and lead with purpose. These values have not only shaped the culture of Google but have also influenced the broader tech industry, showing that it is possible to balance business success with a deep sense of responsibility toward employees, consumers, and society.

Empathy: Leading with Understanding

Sundar Pichai's leadership style is often described as empathetic, a quality that is not always seen in Silicon Valley's often aggressive corporate environment. Pichai's empathetic approach manifests itself in the way he interacts with people, whether they are employees, stakeholders, or even customers. He is known for listening carefully, taking the time to understand different perspectives, and finding ways to address concerns with compassion and fairness. This ability to connect with people on a human level is one of the most striking aspects of his leadership.

One of the most well-known examples of Pichai's empathy came during a difficult time for Google in 2018. A group of employees staged a walkout in protest against the company's handling of sexual harassment allegations. The protests were sparked by revelations that Google had paid out large sums in severance packages to high-ranking executives who had been accused of misconduct. As the leader of the company, Pichai was faced with the delicate task of addressing both the concerns of his employees and the need to maintain Google's reputation.

Rather than dismissing the protests or brushing them aside, Pichai took the time to listen to the concerns of the employees involved. He expressed understanding and supported the need for changes in the company's policies. He acknowledged the emotional toll the issue had taken on employees and pledged to create a safer and more transparent environment for everyone at Google. His approach to the situation highlighted his belief that leadership is about more than making decisions — it's about making people feel heard and valued.

This commitment to empathy is reflected in Pichai's day-to-day leadership as well. He is known for taking the time to connect with employees at all levels of the company. Whether through regular town halls, small group discussions, or one-on-one meetings, Pichai fosters an open, transparent dialogue between leadership and staff. His calm demeanor and thoughtful responses create an environment where people feel comfortable sharing their ideas and concerns.

Pichai's empathy is also evident in the way he manages conflict within the company. In the fast-paced world of tech, disagreements are inevitable. However, Pichai has consistently shown a remarkable ability to navigate these conflicts with tact, ensuring that different viewpoints are heard and that the company's values are always maintained. This has created a culture at Google where employees feel safe to voice dissenting opinions without fear of retribution, a rare and valuable trait in today's corporate world.

Innovation: Fostering a Culture of Creativity

Innovation is the heart of Google, and Sundar Pichai has always believed that a company's ability to innovate is directly tied to the freedom it gives its employees to experiment, explore new ideas, and take risks. As a leader, Pichai has been a vocal advocate for creating a work environment that encourages creative thinking and embraces failure as a stepping stone to success.

One of the most significant aspects of Pichai's leadership in this area is his focus on collaborative innovation. He understands that the best ideas often emerge from diverse perspectives and cross-disciplinary collaboration. At Google, this belief has manifested in numerous ways, from the company's 20% time policy (which allowed employees to spend one day a week working on side projects) to the creation of Google X, the company's innovation lab, where engineers and scientists are encouraged to tackle "moonshot" projects, such as the development of Project Loon (which aims to provide internet to remote areas via high-altitude balloons) and Waymo (the self-driving car project).

Pichai's own role in fostering innovation at Google began early in his career. He was a key player in the development of Google Chrome, which started as a project in a small, isolated team. Pichai gave his engineers the freedom to experiment and explore new ways of building a web browser, free from the constraints of traditional corporate hierarchies. The result was one of the most successful products in Google's history, transforming the way millions of people use the internet. It was Pichai's unwavering belief in the power of creative freedom that helped drive the project to success.

However, Pichai's commitment to innovation goes beyond product development. As CEO of Alphabet, he has sought to position the company as a leader not just in technology but in solving global challenges through innovation. Under his leadership, Alphabet has expanded its focus to artificial intelligence, sustainability, and healthcare — areas where the company can make a meaningful impact on society. Pichai's ability to balance business objectives with the desire to solve important societal problems reflects his long-term vision for the role that innovation can play in shaping the future.

Moreover, Pichai has been a firm believer in open-source collaboration, recognizing that the best technological advancements often come when the world's brightest minds work together. Google's support for open-source projects has allowed thousands of developers and engineers around the world to contribute to products like Android and TensorFlow. By championing an open and inclusive approach to innovation, Pichai has helped Google maintain its position at the forefront of technological progress.

Integrity: Leading with a Strong Moral Compass

Integrity has always been a cornerstone of Sundar Pichai's leadership philosophy. In an era when tech giants are often scrutinized for their business practices, Pichai's commitment to ethics and transparency has been a defining feature of his tenure as CEO. He has consistently prioritized doing what is right over what is easy, maintaining Google's commitment to its mission of organizing the world's information in a way that is both helpful and ethical.

One of the clearest demonstrations of Pichai's commitment to integrity came in 2019 when Google faced intense criticism over its handling of user data and its potential role in spreading misinformation. Pichai responded by being transparent about the company's practices and reinforcing Google's responsibility to protect user privacy. He acknowledged the growing concerns around data privacy and pledged to take stronger steps to give users more control over their personal information.

Another example of Pichai's integrity can be seen in his approach to employee well-being. Google has long been known for offering generous benefits, but under Pichai's leadership, the company has taken additional steps to ensure that its employees are not only well-compensated but also supported in their personal and professional growth. Pichai's open-door policy and focus on maintaining a healthy work-life balance are integral to creating a work environment where employees feel valued and respected.

Pichai has also taken a strong stance on diversity and inclusion. While diversity in tech has been a topic of conversation for many years, Pichai has worked to implement tangible changes at Google, including increasing the representation of women and underrepresented minorities in technical roles. His commitment to diversity and inclusion is not just about achieving quotas but about creating a culture where everyone feels empowered to contribute and succeed.

Moreover, Pichai has been a vocal advocate for corporate responsibility in the tech industry. He has often spoken about the importance of using technology to serve the public good and ensuring that companies like Google are held accountable for their actions. This commitment to corporate integrity is part of what makes Pichai one of the most respected leaders in the tech industry today.

Conclusion: The Heart of Sundar Pichai's Leadership

Sundar Pichai's leadership philosophy is built on a foundation of empathy, innovation, and integrity. His approach is a testament to the idea that successful leadership is not just about achieving business goals but about creating an environment where people are valued, creativity is nurtured, and ethical behavior is upheld. Through his leadership, Pichai has transformed Google into not just a tech company but a company that embodies a set of values that extend far beyond the boardroom. His commitment to these principles will undoubtedly continue to shape Google and the tech industry for years to come.

Chapter 8

Navigating Challenges – Resilience in the Face of Adversity

Sundar Pichai's career has been one of exceptional success, yet like all great leaders, he has faced numerous challenges. From navigating the complexities of an evolving tech landscape to managing internal company tensions and external crises, Pichai has consistently demonstrated resilience and an ability to remain calm under pressure. His approach to overcoming adversity has not only shaped his career but also defined his leadership style. This chapter explores some of the most defining challenges Pichai has faced and how these experiences have influenced his philosophy of leadership, decision-making, and problem-solving.

The Early Struggles: From Madurai to IIT Kharagpur

Before Pichai became the leader of one of the world's largest tech companies, he faced challenges that tested his resolve. Growing up in Madurai, India, in a middle-class family, Pichai encountered obstacles that many aspiring leaders face in the early stages of life. His parents, both educated and ambitious for their son's future, placed a strong emphasis on education. Yet, the path to success was not always straightforward. Sundar's early life was marked by the financial constraints that often accompany middle-class families in India, a country where opportunities can sometimes feel out of reach.

Pichai's resilience was first truly tested when he made the decision to pursue a career in engineering. He sought admission to the prestigious Indian Institute of Technology (IIT) Kharagpur, one of the toughest academic institutions in India. The rigorous admission process was a daunting challenge in itself, with a highly competitive entrance exam. Sundar's determination to succeed despite the intense competition in a crowded educational system set the tone for his later career. He poured all his effort into his studies, working tirelessly to make the cut.

At IIT Kharagpur, Pichai was exposed to the rigors of academic life on a new level. The pressure to succeed was immense, but he embraced it. Though he was thousands of miles from home, he found solace in the discipline of his studies, particularly in the areas of materials science and semiconductor physics. His success at IIT, where he earned a degree in metallurgical engineering, was not only the result of intelligence but also of perseverance. He learned early on that resilience, combined with a relentless pursuit of excellence, was the key to overcoming adversity.

The Transition to Silicon Valley: Breaking Into the Tech World

Sundar Pichai's decision to move to the United States and pursue graduate studies at Stanford University was another pivotal moment in his career. Although Pichai had excelled in India, the competitive nature of Silicon Valley posed a new kind of challenge. At Stanford, Pichai encountered a different level of ambition, one that was both exhilarating and daunting. The people around him were some of the brightest minds in the world, and the pressure to succeed was intense.

In 1995, after completing his MBA at the Wharton School of the University of Pennsylvania, Pichai faced a critical decision. Despite offers from various companies, he chose to join Applied Materials, a semiconductor company. While his early career in this space gave him a solid foundation, Pichai's eventual transition to Google in 2004 would prove to be the most defining challenge of his professional life — one that would test his resilience in new and unexpected ways.

Joining Google: From Product Manager to CEO

Sundar Pichai joined Google in 2004, initially focusing on the development of the Google Toolbar. At the time, Google was primarily known for its search engine, and the company's core product offerings were limited. However, Pichai quickly identified opportunities to expand Google's product portfolio. He played a critical role in the development of Google Chrome, a product that would go on to revolutionize the browser market.

At the time, launching a new browser was an enormous challenge. Internet Explorer dominated the market, and many believed that the browser space was already saturated. However, Pichai's resilience shone through. He pushed through internal skepticism and external doubts, leveraging his deep understanding of technology to create a browser that was fast, secure, and user-friendly. When Chrome was launched in 2008, it was a groundbreaking product that forever changed the browser landscape. Despite facing fierce competition from established players like Microsoft, Pichai's innovation and perseverance ultimately paid off.

The development of Google Chrome was not without its challenges. Pichai and his team had to address numerous technical hurdles, including issues with speed, security, and compatibility with existing software. Moreover, they faced the daunting task of convincing users to switch from their current browsers, something that many considered to be a difficult, if not impossible, feat. Yet, Pichai's resilience was key to overcoming these obstacles. He stayed focused on the product's potential, iterating quickly and learning from feedback. The success of Google Chrome became a testament to Pichai's ability to navigate challenges through determination and a deep belief in his product.

Leading Google Through Crisis: The Antitrust Investigations

In the years that followed his success with Chrome, Sundar Pichai's leadership would be tested by an entirely different set of challenges — the increasing scrutiny and regulatory pressure on Google. As Google's products grew to become integral to everyday life, the company began to attract the attention of governments around the world, particularly in the area of antitrust investigations.

In the U.S. and Europe, regulators raised concerns about Google's dominance in search, advertising, and other key areas. The company faced multiple legal challenges, and Pichai found himself at the center of these discussions as the CEO of Google. For many CEOs, such challenges can create a crisis of leadership, as they threaten the very existence of the company. However, Pichai approached these investigations with a combination of transparency and measured calm. He remained focused on ensuring that Google's core values of providing useful and unbiased information were not compromised by the scrutiny of regulators.

Despite the external pressures, Pichai's approach was characterized by resilience and a deep sense of responsibility. He advocated for policies that would protect user privacy and championed the role that Google played in fostering competition in the tech industry. Pichai was able to navigate these challenges with a steady hand, focusing on long-term goals and using his diplomatic skills to address the concerns of regulators while maintaining Google's commitment to innovation.

The Leadership Challenge of Becoming CEO of Alphabet

In 2015, Pichai was appointed the CEO of Google's parent company, Alphabet, marking a significant milestone in his career. However, becoming the CEO of such a vast and multifaceted organization brought its own set of challenges. Under Pichai's leadership, Alphabet was dealing with the complexities of being both a tech company and a conglomerate with diverse interests, including self-driving cars (Waymo), healthcare (Verily), and more.

One of the key challenges Pichai faced was integrating these disparate projects under the Alphabet umbrella while maintaining the innovative spirit that defined Google. The company was not only expanding its product offerings but also venturing into industries where it had no prior experience. Pichai's ability to balance these new initiatives while continuing to drive the growth of Google's core businesses was a testament to his adaptability and resilience.

Pichai also had to manage internal challenges, such as dealing with employee unrest over issues like the company's handling of sexual harassment allegations. In 2018, a large group of Google employees staged a walkout, demanding changes to the company's handling of sexual harassment claims. Pichai was thrust into a difficult position, balancing the concerns of his employees with the need to protect the company's culture. In response, Pichai acknowledged the mistakes that had been made, apologized to the employees, and promised reforms, demonstrating a willingness to confront difficult issues head-on.

Resilience in the Face of Personal Loss

Beyond his professional challenges, Sundar Pichai's resilience has been shaped by personal adversity. In 2020, Pichai faced the loss of his beloved father, a man who had been a significant influence on his life and career. Despite the emotional toll, Pichai continued to lead Alphabet with focus and grace, keeping his commitments to the company and its employees while privately mourning the loss.

Pichai's ability to navigate both personal and professional challenges has been an essential aspect of his leadership style. He has always demonstrated that resilience is not just about weathering external storms but about facing personal difficulties with dignity and strength, while still fulfilling one's obligations.

Conclusion: The Power of Resilience in Leadership

Throughout his career, Sundar Pichai has faced a wide array of challenges that have tested his resilience, decision-making skills, and leadership abilities. From the early days of his education in India to his rise as the CEO of Alphabet, Pichai's ability to navigate adversity with composure and determination has defined his career. Whether dealing with technical hurdles, regulatory challenges, or personal loss, Pichai's resilience has not only shaped his leadership approach but also solidified his reputation as a steady and principled leader.

In the face of adversity, Pichai has demonstrated that resilience is not about avoiding challenges, but about embracing them, learning from them, and growing stronger in the process. His ability to remain calm under pressure, maintain focus on long-term goals, and inspire those around him is what sets him apart as a leader. Sundar Pichai's career serves as a powerful reminder that adversity, when approached with resilience, can be a catalyst for growth and transformation.

Chapter 10

Legacy and Impact – Inspiring the Next Generation

Sundar Pichai's journey from a small town in Madurai, India, to becoming the CEO of Google and Alphabet is nothing short of extraordinary. Over the course of his career, Pichai has not only transformed the tech industry but has also redefined what it means to be a leader in today's fast-paced, ever-evolving world. His legacy is built on his commitment to innovation, his ethical approach to leadership, and his ability to navigate the complexities of both the tech landscape and global society. As Pichai continues to shape the future of technology, his story serves as an inspiration to future generations of leaders, innovators, and dreamers who seek to make their mark on the world.

Transforming the Tech Industry: The Google Revolution

One of the most profound ways in which Sundar Pichai has left his mark on the world is through his leadership at Google. His role in developing groundbreaking products like Google Chrome, Android, and Google Drive has revolutionized the way people access and interact with information. These innovations have become integral parts of daily life for billions of users worldwide, and their impact is felt in nearly every aspect of modern society.

Pichai's contributions to Google's evolution have been pivotal in solidifying the company's dominance in the tech industry. Under his leadership, Google expanded its reach into artificial intelligence, cloud computing, and self-driving cars, and more. These innovations are not just about making technology more advanced; they are about creating systems that improve lives and address global challenges. For example, Google's AI-driven projects have the potential to change industries such as healthcare, education, and transportation, making them more efficient, accessible, and equitable.

However, Pichai's legacy extends beyond the products themselves. He has been a champion of open-source innovation, ensuring that Google's technology is not just a proprietary advantage but also a tool that can be used by millions of developers around the world. Through his efforts, he has fostered a culture of collaboration, encouraging innovation to thrive not only within Google but also within the global tech ecosystem. The legacy of an interconnected, collaborative, and open tech community is something that Pichai has helped to create and continues to nurture.

Ethical Leadership: A New Era of Responsibility

Beyond his technical accomplishments, Pichai's approach to leadership stands as a beacon of ethical responsibility in an industry often criticized for its lack of accountability. From his early days at Google, Pichai has made it clear that success should not come at the expense of ethics. His belief in the importance of integrity, transparency, and social responsibility has been a hallmark of his leadership style.

Pichai has frequently championed privacy and data security, advocating for stronger protections for users in an age where personal information is often exploited for commercial gain. Under his leadership, Google has made significant strides in offering more user control over data and prioritizing security. At the same time, Pichai has emphasized the importance of sustainability, not only within Google's operations but also across the tech industry as a whole. Google has committed to achieving carbon neutrality and is working on projects that aim to tackle climate change through the use of AI and machine learning.

Pichai's leadership has set a new standard for what ethical responsibility should look like in tech companies. His willingness to address sensitive issues such as employee well-being, diversity, and inclusion head-on is a testament to his commitment to creating a work environment that fosters fairness, respect, and opportunity for all. His approach to leadership is a reminder that businesses — especially those in the tech industry — must act as stewards of society, using their resources and influence to create positive change.

Global Innovation: A Vision for the Future

Perhaps one of the most defining aspects of Sundar Pichai's legacy is his ability to think globally. As CEO of Alphabet, Pichai has consistently demonstrated a keen understanding of the importance of technology in addressing global challenges. His vision is not just about advancing technology for its own sake but about leveraging that technology to create solutions that can improve the lives of people around the world.

One of Pichai's key initiatives has been the development of Google's AI-powered products aimed at improving access to education and healthcare in underserved communities. His belief in the power of technology to level the playing field is central to his approach to global innovation. For Pichai, the goal of innovation is not just to create cutting-edge products but to ensure that those products benefit everyone, regardless of location or socio-economic status.

Through projects like Google's Project Loon, which aims to provide internet access to remote and rural areas through high-altitude balloons, and Google.org, the company's philanthropic arm, Pichai has demonstrated that technology can be a force for good. His commitment to global expansion, paired with his focus on inclusivity, ensures that the tech industry will continue to drive positive change for years to come.

Inspiring the Next Generation: A Leader for Tomorrow

As Sundar Pichai looks to the future, his story continues to serve as a powerful inspiration to future generations of leaders and innovators. Pichai's journey is a testament to the power of perseverance, resilience, and the pursuit of excellence. From his humble beginnings in Madurai to his rise as the CEO of one of the world's most influential companies, Pichai has shown that with determination, vision, and a commitment to doing what's right, anything is possible.

For aspiring leaders, Pichai's example offers valuable lessons in empathy, integrity, and the importance of creating inclusive spaces for innovation. His ability to listen to others, foster collaboration, and lead with a strong moral compass makes him a role model for anyone who seeks to lead with purpose and responsibility. Moreover, his focus on building bridges across cultures and his belief in the transformative power of technology serve as a reminder that the challenges we face today can be overcome through collective effort and forward-thinking innovation.

For future innovators, Pichai's legacy underscores the importance of thinking big and being willing to take risks. Whether in technology, business, or any other field, Pichai's career illustrates that true innovation comes from the willingness to tackle difficult problems, challenge the status quo, and never stop learning. His story encourages young minds to push boundaries, explore new ideas, and always remain curious about the world around them.

In the years to come, Sundar Pichai's impact will continue to be felt in every corner of the world. His leadership and vision will continue to shape the future of technology and business, inspiring the next generation of innovators, entrepreneurs, and leaders who will build on the foundation he has laid.

Conclusion: A Legacy of Leadership and Vision

Sundar Pichai's legacy is one of visionary leadership, boundless innovation, and unwavering commitment to creating a better future. His impact on the tech industry, his approach to ethical leadership, and his global vision have not only transformed Google and Alphabet but have also left an indelible mark on the world. As we look to the future, Pichai's journey serves as a powerful reminder that the path to success is not defined solely by what you achieve but by how you choose to lead, innovate, and inspire others along the way.

In the end, Sundar Pichai's legacy will be remembered not only for the incredible technologies he has helped create but for the profound and lasting impact he has had on leadership practices and global innovation. His story will continue to inspire generations of leaders to come, guiding them to build a better, more inclusive, and more innovative world.

Conclusion

The Journey Continues – What Lies Ahead for Sundar Pichai

As Sundar Pichai's remarkable journey unfolds, it is clear that his story is far from over. From his humble beginnings in Madurai to steering Alphabet into a new era of innovation, Pichai has already made an indelible mark on the world of technology and leadership. But as with all true visionaries, his work is never done. The future holds vast opportunities for Pichai, Alphabet, and the tech industry as a whole — opportunities that will continue to shape the world for generations to come.

Paving the Way for Alphabet's Future

Under Pichai's leadership, Alphabet has already established itself as a diversified tech conglomerate, with interests spanning beyond Google's core business of search and advertising. From self-driving cars through Waymo to the advancements in artificial intelligence and quantum computing, Alphabet is well-positioned to continue its role as a global leader in tech. However, Pichai's vision suggests that the company is only at the beginning of a much larger transformation.

In the coming years, Alphabet is expected to double down on its focus on artificial intelligence (AI) and machine learning. Pichai has long been a proponent of the potential of AI to solve some of the world's most pressing challenges, from climate change to healthcare to education. As AI continues to advance, Alphabet is likely to take bold steps in leveraging this technology to drive breakthroughs in areas such as personalized medicine, automated healthcare, sustainability, and global connectivity. The role of AI in addressing global inequality and improving life for marginalized communities could become one of Alphabet's key missions, with Pichai at the helm ensuring that these advancements are not only innovative but also ethical and inclusive.

Moreover, Alphabet's commitment to sustainability will likely take on even greater urgency. As the world grapples with climate change, Pichai's leadership will likely drive initiatives that harness the power of AI to reduce emissions, promote renewable energy, and create sustainable solutions for both individuals and businesses. Alphabet's goal of operating entirely on renewable energy by 2025 is just the beginning. As the world's tech industry leaders look for ways to mitigate their environmental impact, Sundar Pichai's vision will undoubtedly be a guiding light, driving the next wave of green technology and eco-friendly innovations.

Another area where Pichai's future impact may be significant is in the evolving space of global digital infrastructure. In the coming years, Alphabet may expand its role in providing internet access to underserved populations, particularly in remote and rural areas. Project Loon and similar initiatives show how Pichai's vision could expand to ensure that the next billion people are connected, bridging the digital divide and bringing the benefits of the internet to people who have long been excluded from its advantages. His leadership could lead Alphabet to develop a new suite of technologies that not only improve internet access but also provide access to education, health resources, and job opportunities, further contributing to global economic development.

What Lies Ahead for Sundar Pichai?

As Sundar Pichai looks ahead, it is clear that his legacy is far from being fully written. Under his leadership, Alphabet has become not just a tech company, but a driving force of global change. And as the tech industry continues to evolve, Pichai's leadership will continue to be a beacon guiding it toward greater responsibility, inclusivity, and sustainability.

While Pichai has already revolutionized industries such as search, advertising, mobile computing, and web browsers, the next chapter in his journey will likely involve steering the company into even more groundbreaking fields. Quantum computing, a domain that promises to revolutionize industries ranging from pharmaceuticals to finance, will likely be a key focus. Alphabet has already invested heavily in quantum research through its Google Quantum AI lab, and Pichai is likely to lead efforts in pushing the limits of what is possible with this next-generation computing technology.

Additionally, Pichai's attention will likely turn more deeply toward the metaverse and virtual reality. As companies begin to invest in creating more immersive digital worlds,

Pichai's vision of creating scalable, ethical technologies will be crucial in shaping this next frontier. Under his guidance, Alphabet could define the future of how individuals interact with both the physical and digital worlds, ensuring that such experiences are designed with a focus on user well-being, privacy, and inclusivity.

The Enduring Lessons: Resilience, Empathy, and Innovation

As we reflect on Pichai's journey, several enduring lessons stand out — lessons that will continue to inspire generations of leaders, innovators, and entrepreneurs across the globe.

The first of these is resilience. Throughout his career, Pichai has demonstrated an unwavering ability to face challenges head-on. From overcoming early struggles in his personal life to navigating the pressures of leading one of the world's most influential companies, his resilience has been a cornerstone of his success. For future leaders, Pichai's example teaches that the path to greatness is often paved with adversity, but it is in how we respond to those challenges that we find our true strength.

Another key lesson from Pichai's journey is the power of empathy in leadership. Pichai's leadership style is characterized by a profound empathy for people — both within Google and the broader global community. His decision to prioritize employee well-being, promote diversity and inclusion, and ensure that technological advancements benefit society reflects his deep belief that success is not just about business outcomes but about improving lives. For future leaders, Pichai exemplifies the importance of leading with both head and heart.

Lastly, innovation is at the core of Pichai's legacy. His relentless pursuit of new ideas and solutions has not only propelled

Alphabet to unprecedented heights but has also redefined industries. Future innovators can take inspiration from Pichai's commitment to continuous learning and his willingness to challenge the status quo. He reminds us that true innovation comes not from playing it safe, but from daring to think differently and solve problems that have never been solved before.

The Future is Bright

As Sundar Pichai looks to the future, he remains firmly focused on creating technologies that have the power to change the world. His leadership will continue to shape the next era of innovation, ensuring that Alphabet remains at the forefront of technological advancements while staying true to its core values of integrity, responsibility, and inclusivity. The challenges of tomorrow are vast, but with leaders like Pichai at the helm, we can be confident that the journey ahead will be one of transformation, opportunity, and positive global impact.

Sundar Pichai's story is a powerful reminder that the future is not something we wait for — it is something we create. As we move into this next chapter, Pichai's legacy will continue to inspire and guide future generations of leaders, innovators, and dreamers who will build on the foundation he has laid.

Printed in Great Britain
by Amazon

62695510R00067